Reading and Learning from Informational Text

by Jennifer L. Harner

CHERRY LAKE PUBLISHING · ANN ARBOR, MICHIGAN

A NOTE TO PARENTS AND TEACHERS: Please remind your children how to stay safe online before they do the activities in this book.

A NOTE TO KIDS: Always remember your safety comes first!

Cherry Lake Publishing

Published in the United States of America
by Cherry Lake Publishing
Ann Arbor, Michigan
www.cherrylakepublishing.com

Content Adviser: Gail Dickinson, PhD, Associate Professor,
Old Dominion University, Norfolk, Virginia

Photo Credits: Cover, ©iStockphoto.com/alejandrophotography; page 5, ©Yuri Arcurs/Shutterstock, Inc.; page 6, ©Monkey Business Images/Shutterstock, Inc.; page 9, ©Dawn Shearer-Simonetti/Shutterstock, Inc.; page 10, ©Vietrov Dmytro/Shutterstock, Inc.; page 14, ©JJ pixs/Shutterstock, Inc.; page 17, ©iofoto/ Shutterstock, Inc.

Library of Congress Cataloging-in-Publication Data
Harner, Jennifer L.
Reading and learning from informational text / By Jennifer L. Harner.
pages cm. – (Information Explorer Junior)
Includes bibliographical references and index.
ISBN 978-1-62431-134-5 (lib. bdg.) – ISBN 978-1-62431-200-7 (e-book) –
ISBN 978-1-62431-266-3 (pbk.)
1. Reading (Primary) 2. Reading comprehension—Juvenile literature. I. Title.
LB1525.H24 2013
372.4–dc23 2013005814

Cherry Lake Publishing would like to acknowledge the work of The Partnership for 21st Century Skills. Please visit *www.p21.org* for more information.

Printed in the United States of America
Corporate Graphics Inc.
July 2013
CLFA13

Table of Contents

CHAPTER ONE

What Is Informational Text?

Do you read a storybook to learn new things? No! You look for informational text. Informational text is filled with useful facts, figures, and instructions. There are many kinds of informational books. Biographies contain information about a person. Encyclopedias have articles about many different topics. Dictionaries contain information about words.

Books aren't the only place you can find informational text. Newspapers and

A recipe can help you learn how to make new kinds of food.

magazines also contain informational text. Instruction manuals tell you how to build a toy or play a game. Informational text can come in printed and digital formats. Many Web sites and **databases** are full of informational text.

A newspaper is an informational text that can help you learn about current events.

Informational text is just what it sounds like. It is text that teaches you or gives you information. The book you are reading right now is an informational text. It contains information about informational text!

Try This

Answers to questions are found in many different types of informational text sources. Some answers might be found in books. Some might be found online. Some might be found in other sources. Which types of text could help answer these questions?

1. What did Thomas Jefferson do to help his country?
2. Who invented the airplane?
3. What is happening in my town this week?
4. How do I make chocolate chip cookies?
5. How do I put this toy together?

Answers: 1. Biography, 2. Book or Web site about airplanes, 3. Newspaper, 4. Cookbook, 5. Instruction manual

To get a copy of this activity, visit www.cherrylakepublishing.com/activities.

Chapter Two: Learning from Informational Text

CHAPTER TWO

Learning from Informational Text

You always start at the beginning when you read a story. Then you read to the end. **Comprehending** informational text is a little different. You don't always need to read informational text from beginning to end. You can use different **strategies** to find the facts you need. One strategy is to use chapter titles. They point you toward where to find the information you want. They can help you figure out which questions will be answered in each chapter.

You might need more than one book to make sure your information is correct.

Do you think you have found an answer to your question? Check to make sure it is correct. One way to check your answer is to look at more than one text. Are the answers the same? This means your information is probably correct. Are they different? This means you should check a third text. This new text may give you the same answer as one of the others. This means that answer is likely to be correct.

Another strategy is to check the **copyright dates** of your sources. Some information changes often. Newer texts will give you the latest updates. You might want to know how many people live in the United States. More people live in the United States now than in the past. A book from 1992 will have different information than a book from last year.

Always use a new book when you need up-to-date information.

Try This

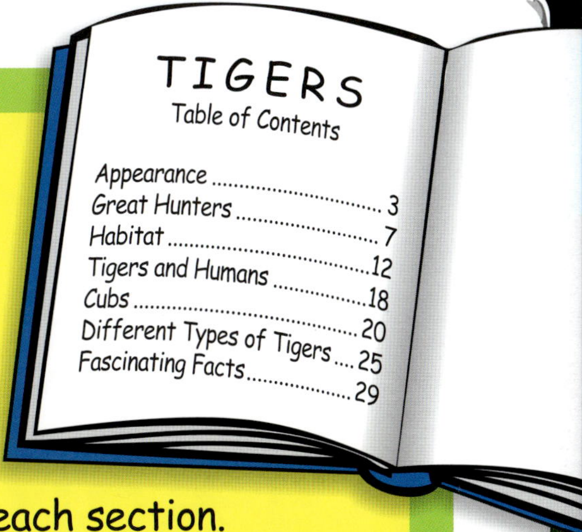

Look at the chapter titles of an informational text. Use them to ask questions about each section. Can you answer the questions after reading the chapter? This means you understood the text! Which chapter would you check to answer these questions?

1. How old are tigers when they leave their mothers?
2. Where do tigers live?
3. What is the difference between a Bengal tiger and a Siberian tiger?
4. What do tigers look like?
5. How have humans caused problems for tigers in the wild?

Try writing a research question that might be answered in the "Appearance" chapter.

Answers: 1. Cubs, 2. Habitat, 3. Different Types of Tigers, 4. Appearance, 5. Tigers and Humans

To get a copy of this activity, visit www.cherrylakepublishing.com/activities.

CHAPTER THREE

Getting Organized

Informational text often includes special features. These features help you find and comprehend information. Text features organize the text and highlight important information. They also provide visuals to help you understand what you are reading. Some common text features include page numbers, indexes, and tables of contents.

The most basic organizational feature is page numbering. Page numbers sometimes appear in storybooks. They are much more important in informational text, though. Page numbers are used in the table of contents in the front of the book. They are

The table of contents is the first place you should look when you need certain information.

also used in the index at the end of the book. These features help you quickly find the information you need. A table of contents displays the general layout of how the information in the book is organized. The index is more specific. It leads you to the exact pages where topics are discussed.

Organizational text features are different for online sources. You probably won't see

Online sources are organized differently than printed sources.

numbered pages. There will instead be a menu with **links** to different sections of text. Clicking on a link brings you to a new page or file.

Print and electronic resources both have headings throughout the text. Headings are titles for smaller chunks of text. They are similar to chapter titles. They make it easier for you to skim the text for the information you need.

Try This

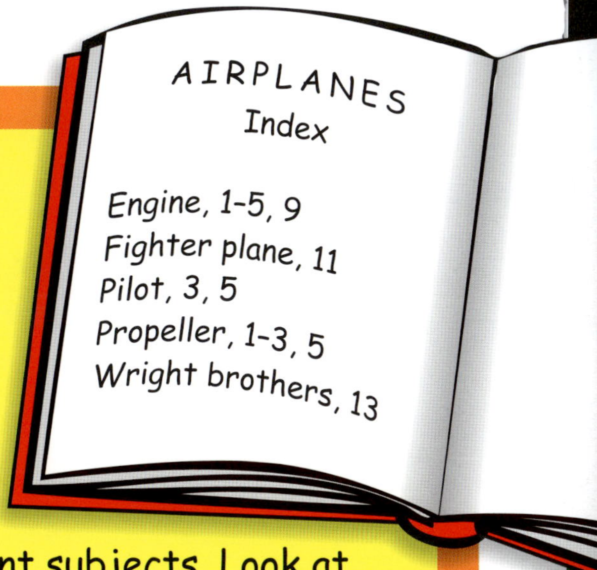

Using an index can save you time by directing you to pages that contain information about different subjects. Look at the index above. Which pages could answer the research questions below?

1. How do propellers work?
2. When did the Wright brothers make the first successful airplane flight?
3. What makes fighter planes special?
4. How are pilots trained?
5. How do engines keep airplanes in the air?

Answers: 1. 1-3, 5; 2. 13; 3. 11; 4. 3, 5; 5. 1-5, 9

To get a copy of this activity, visit www.cherrylakepublishing.com/activities.

CHAPTER FOUR

Information from Visuals

Sometimes information is easier to understand if it is presented visually. California is about 2,800 miles (4,500 kilometers) from Maryland. Understanding this information as text can be difficult. But seeing the distance on a map with a **scale** makes it easier to understand.

Images can also help you understand what you are reading. Words can describe a tiger's black and orange stripes. But a picture can show exactly what they look like. **Captions** next to a picture explain what you are seeing.

Authors use tables or graphs to help you understand facts involving numbers.

A table of animals and the names for their babies can give you information more quickly than a paragraph can. Imagine you want to compare the populations of different states. It would likely be easier to understand the information in graph form.

Maps are one kind of visual feature you are likely to find in informational texts.

To get a copy of this activity, visit www.cherrylakepublishing.com/activities.

Try This

Informational text shares facts in many ways. Use the chart and graph to answer the questions below.

State	Capital
Arizona	Phoenix
Delaware	Dover
Maryland	Annapolis
Pennsylvania	Harrisburg

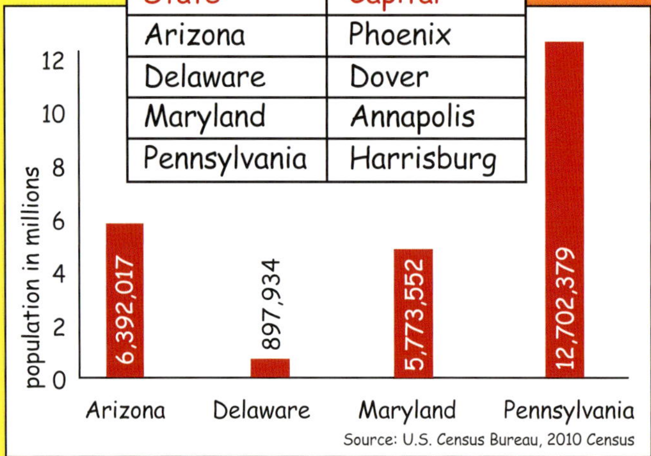

1. What is the capital of Maryland?
2. Harrisburg is the capital of what state?
3. Which state has Phoenix as a capital?
4. How many people lived in Delaware in 2010?
5. Which of these states was home to more than 10 million people in 2010?

Answers: 1. Annapolis, 2. Pennsylvania, 3. Arizona, 4. 897,934, 5. Pennsylvania

CHAPTER FIVE

Identifying Important Information

Some text features highlight especially interesting information. These features help you identify some of the most important information in the text. Keywords are often in bold print or highlighted. This makes the words stand out. It also lets you know that you can find those words in the book's glossary. A glossary is like a small dictionary. It is made just for the text you are reading. It keeps you from having to look up words in a separate dictionary.

Sidebars are another way of highlighting important information. Sidebars are in a box

alongside the main text. They may contain a closer look at something mentioned in the text. They might share information related to the main topic. Sometimes they are colored to stand out even more.

You will use a variety of informational texts in your life. They will help you work on school projects. They will also enable you to learn new things on your own. The strategies you learned in this book can help you the next time you need to answer a question or learn something new!

To get a copy of this activity, visit www.cherrylakepublishing.com/activities.

Try This

Look at the Web site below. It has examples of many different text features. Which ones can you identify?

1. Caption
2. Sidebar
3. Menu
4. Photograph
5. Heading
6. Map
7. Article Title

Which text features are there to organize the information? Which point out important information? Which show information in a visual way?

Glossary

captions (KAP-shuhnz) explanations or descriptions that go with photographs or illustrations

comprehending (kahm-pre-HEN-ding) understanding fully

copyright dates (KAH-pee-rite DAYTS) dates on an informational text that show when it was created or published

databases (DAY-tuh-bay-siz) sets of related information that are organized and stored in a computer

links (LINGKS) connections between Web pages or Web sites that allow you to jump from one to another with a single mouse click

scale (SKALE) the ratio between the measurements on a map or model and the actual measurements

strategies (STRAT-uh-jeez) clever plans for achieving a goal

Find Out More

BOOKS

Fontichiaro, Kristin. *Find Out Firsthand: Using Primary Sources.* Ann Arbor, MI: Cherry Lake Publishing, 2013.

Truesdell, Ann. *Find the Facts with Encyclopedias.* Ann Arbor, MI: Cherry Lake Publishing, 2012.

Truesdell, Ann. *Get to the Right Site.* Ann Arbor, MI: Cherry Lake Publishing, 2012.

WEB SITES

American Association of School Librarians—KidsConnect's Research Toolbox

www.ala.org/aasl/aboutaasl/aaslcommunity/quicklinks/k12students/aaslkctools

Learn how to come up with good research questions and search for quality informational texts.

Kentucky Virtual Library—How to Do Research

www.kyvl.org/kids/homebase.html

Check out some helpful tips for doing research and using different kinds of informational text.

Index

About the Author

Jenny Harner is a national board certified media specialist in Maryland. She and her husband, Mike, enjoy traveling and spending time with their son, Derek, and cat, Moose.